WHAT IF WE HAVE IT ALL WRONG ABOUT GOD?

*From the moment Satan caused Adam and Eve
to become afraid of God in the Garden of Eden
after they had eaten the forbidden fruit until today,
his greatest weapon of mass destruction is to deceive people
into having a wrong perception of God and how He sees and relates to us.*

What if we have it all wrong about God?

Q: IN YOUR PERCEPTION OF GOD, HOW DOES HE SEE YOU? HOW DO YOU
SEE HIM? IF YOU DESCRIBE GOD IN ONE WORD, WHAT WOULD THAT BE?

The Bible says, "God is love." (See 1 John 4.8) How could pure love produce anything that contradicted love? The mixture would render it impure. Our God is pure love personified and everything about Him must be understood from that vantage point.

The grace of God will continually appear to become bigger and more beautiful as we grow. Grace is the expression of Love Himself. Jesus Christ is the source and center of everything we can know about our Father. (See Hebrews 1: 3) Surely, our concept of God must be the starting point because it will inform our beliefs about every other biblical topic.

Growing things change, and that includes people. If any of us still believes exactly the way we have always believed, one might be justified in asking if we have grown at all. When we confidently believe what we believe, it can be a real challenge to recognize and acknowledge that we may not have it all right.

My prayer is that as we journey together through this conference, the Holy Spirit—the One who Jesus promised would guide us into all truth—will cause us to repent where necessary. To a great extent this is a conference about repentance, a word that literally means, "to change our minds." Compare what you hear here with what the Bible says and ask the Teacher to guide you.

Let us encounter real God in Jesus through the Holy Spirit! Are you ready to be embraced by Him?

GRACE IS A DANCE

Where did you come from? What is your origin?
If you think you can find your origin
in Adam, you aren't looking back far enough.
Your source is the One who set everything in motion
in the beginning— the One who preceded that beginning.
You weren't an impulsive idea your Creator had in time.
He held you dearly in His heart before
He spoke the first molecule into existence!

1. WHAT IS GOD LIKE?

A. God Is a Relationship

The Hebrew word translated "God" is *Elohiym*. The word has great significance.

_____

_____

_____

As three in one, our God is first and foremost relational.

_____

_____

_____

B. "God is love" (1 John 4: 8)

The biblical God is first and foremost One who exists in a loving relationship. That defines Him, so everything we know about Him must fit within that definition.

_____

_____

_____

Our God is a relational God who has eternally lived in a self-sustained communion of love and life existing within Himself. That defines God. Above everything else, He is all about communion, relationship, and interconnectedness—all based on love.

There is no other side to God that Jesus didn't reveal.
"Jesus is the exact representation of [the Father's] nature."
(Hebrews 1: 3)
"He who has seen Me has seen the Father" (John 14: 9).

_____

_____

_____

_____

C. God is the Divine Dance (Perichoresis)

Perichoresis: a community of being in which each person of the Trinity, while maintaining His distinctive identity, shares His very essence with the others. The word denotes a oneness that creates a unified movement of intimate relationship—like a dance. The word perichoresis comes from the words peri and chorein. *Peri* denotes a circle, as in the word "perimeter." *Chorein* means, "to make room for and to enclose." Dancing is a good metaphor for this loving, synchronized movement of the Father, Son, and Spirit enclosed together in one essence.

_____

_____

It might be more accurate to describe Him as a divine Dancer who eternally celebrates love and life in the divine Circle Dance that is Himself.

_____

_____

_____

_____

2. WHY ARE YOU HERE?

Q: Why did God bring you into existence? It was simply to be loved.

In the beauty of the eternal plan, this love finds greater expression in quantity, not quality.

_____

_____

_____

Humanity was created to participate in the great dance.

_____

_____

_____

You are your Father's dream come true! The apostle Paul described us as "God's masterpiece" (Ephesians 2: 10 NLT). You have been embraced and bound up in Jesus Christ and are now His very offspring (see Acts 17: 28).

_____

_____

_____

3. WHAT DID GOD DO?

A. God is the Initiator

Jesus identified His mission, saying, "For the Son of Man has come to seek and to save that which was lost" (Luke 19: 10). It is important to realize that God doesn't wait for us to make a move to resolve our problem of sin. (See Romans 3: 11.)

_____

_____

_____

B. The Word for You

Q: Why is Jesus called "the Word?"

A word exists for the purpose of communicating to another—but each person in the Godhead already fully knows everything the other persons know, so why did this Word exist in the beginning? If Jesus, as the Word, didn't need to communicate anything to the Father or the Spirit, to whom did He have something to communicate? The answer is thrilling. The intended recipient of the Word is you.

_____

_____

_____

C. Being Lost Is All Relative

"Nothing can be lost that is not first owned."

_____

_____

_____

_____

The starting point for the sheep, the coin, and the prodigal wasn't their lostness but their belonging—despite their current status. Notice that in these parables, Jesus never indicates that the shepherd of the lost sheep, the owner of the lost coin, or the father of the lost son were ever angry about the lostness of their treasured possession. Far from it. They were driven by a loving passion to recover what they loved—at any cost.

_____

_____

_____

Lostness has no meaning apart from the reference point of belonging. If belonging didn't come first, nothing could be lost. It's true with humanity itself. Before we were ever lost in Adam, we already belonged in Christ.

ENCOUNTER YOUR REAL GOD

You weren't an impulsive idea your Creator had in time.
Your God held you dearly in His heart before He spoke
the first molecule into existence. YOU ARE SO DEAR to God!

Love is our God's DNA. "God is love"
is the most definitive statement that can be said about Him.

Your God is a relational God who has eternally lived
in a self-sustained communion of love and life existing within Himself.
That defines God. He is all about communion,
relationship, and interconnectedness—all based on love.

There is no dark side to God that Jesus didn't reveal.

You have been set in the place of a child
who is loved and accepted by your Father. We all are here to be loved.

The traditional language of the religious world speaks of finding God,
but the truth is that He is the One who has found us!

SIN IS A SOUR NOTE

*Love always takes the initiative without waiting to see
what its recipient will do first.
From the instant of mankind's creation,
our God's blessings didn't depend on human service toward Him.
God's grace certainly motivates us to honor Him with acts of service,
but His blessings are not the slightest bit contingent
on our service to Him.*

1. GOD'S HEART FOR YOU

A. The heart of our Creator is to bless you.

"Be fruitful!" He said. "Multiply... fill... subdue...rule..." These are the words our generous Father first spoke to those He had given life. Just as His first act reveals His heart, so do His first words to them.

_____

_____

_____

B. The Joy of Creation

Think about a time when you gave a special gift to somebody you particularly love. Our God is a joyful God, a dancing God, even a laughing God. He delights in seeing you happily receiving His love.
(See Zephaniah 3: 17)

_____

_____

_____

2. THE TWO CHOICES

To eat from this tree would give Adam and Eve knowledge of what was right and what was wrong, knowledge they did not initially possess. (Note carefully the name of this tree. It was a tree that gave knowledge, but knowledge of what? It gave knowledge of good and evil, of right and wrong.)

A. Moralism or Union?

Q: Did Adam and Eve need to know good from evil?

Religion is all about right and wrong. These two didn't need to know right from wrong for one simple reason— they lived every moment in the union they shared with their Creator.

_____

_____

Moral dualism focuses on good and evil.

_____

_____

The tree of the knowledge of good and evil can produce moral living, but only union with God can produce the lifestyle He intends for you—a miraculous life.

_____

B. Warning in Love

The first time the subject of sin is mentioned in the Bible, the point God made clear is that sin brings death. Not God, but sin.

_____

_____

God's heart was to protect, not punish.

_____

_____

3. A DIFFERENT DEITY

Satan introduced a false sense of inadequacy within Eve. "I can be like God!" Eve must have thought. "How could it not be a good decision to do anything that would make me more like God?" The fact is, she already was like God in every way that mattered. Objective truth can lose its subjective influence in our lives when we allow ourselves to believe a lie. We can become blind to the truth and dead to the reality of who our Creator has made us to be.

A. Everything Changed

_____

_____

_____

B. We Were There Too

The concept of vicariousness.

_____

_____

When Adam sinned, his vicarious act involved all humanity. The key is that what one person does can affect everybody else.

_____

_____

4. THE CONSEQUENCES

What happened in that moment may well still affect how you think about God right now. Adam believed that because he had done wrong, God would relate to him as an angry judge. Before Adam and Eve sinned, they both saw God as the loving Father that He is, but from the moment they ate from the forbidden tree, their whole perspective of God changed. Since that moment, those blind to the truth still believe God is angered toward us by our wrongdoing.

A. Hiding from an Angry God

God hadn't changed. Adam had.

_____

_____

_____

_____

People may believe God knows about their sin and is angry about it and toward them. So they do exactly what Adam and Eve did—they try to hide.

_____

_____

_____

_____

B. Punishment or Protection?

Q: Why did God drive them from the Garden?

_____

_____

_____

_____

His decision to ban them from the Garden of Eden for their own protection was a mercy shown to them when they didn't even know they needed it.

_____

_____

_____

_____

C. A God Who Keeps Score

Perhaps the greatest ruin that came to mankind in the fall is man's distorted, perverted perception of God.

_____

_____

_____

As a result of Adam's sin, an open, vulnerable, transparent, and intimate relationship with God was replaced with fear, shame, guilt, and a sense of separation between the Creator and His beloved creation.

_____

_____

_____

Which perspective more closely resembles the way you see Him? In your default setting, is He the Father who loves to walk with you, who wants to bless you and see you be fruitful? Or do you see Him as a judge who knows how you've behaved and isn't happy about it? Do you see Him as a Loving Father or more like a moral accountant who is keeping books on your thoughts, feelings, words, and deeds? We can't possibly advance in our own grace walk beyond our concept of God. We will never move further into living in grace unless our concept of God's goodness grows.

ENCOUNTER YOUR REAL GOD

The heart of our Creator is to bless you.

Sin brings death. Not your God, but sin. Sin is a fatal disease.

The focus of people today is all about doing right and avoiding wrong,
but that was not and is not the plan your God has for you.
He has a better plan based on your union with Him through Jesus Christ.

God hadn't changed. Adam had. People may believe
God knows about their sin and is angry about it and toward them.
So they try to hide.

Perhaps the greatest ruin that came to mankind
in the fall is man's distorted, perverted perception of God.

We can't possibly advance in our own grace walk
beyond our concept of God. We will never move further
into living in grace unless our concept of God's goodness grows.

JESUS LIVED AS US

*The Incarnation of God in Jesus
is the greatest moment that has ever occurred in time or eternity.
The word doesn't simply refer to the birth of Jesus,
but to His entire ministry as a human being.*

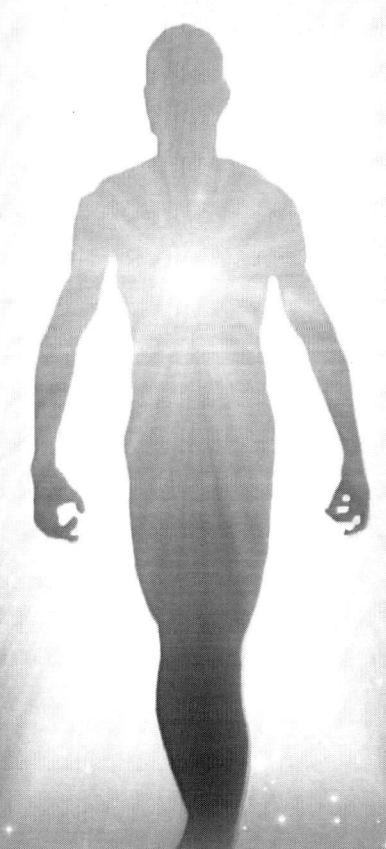

Jesus Lived as Us

1. LOVE INCARNATE

A. The Incarnation

> "The circle wasn't broken by His humanity. Far from it—His becoming a man enlarged the circle so that mankind would be included. He came to us to draw us in." - Athanasius

B. Jesus as the Last Adam

Jesus was and is the divine mediator from both the Godward and human sides.

_____

_____

_____

Jesus didn't just do what He did for us; He did it as us.

_____

_____

_____

C. Jesus Lived for Us

The implications of the vicarious life of Jesus touch every area of our lives.

_____

_____

_____

The life of Jesus has vicarious application to our lives in important ways.

3. VICARIOUS OBEDIENCE

Q: What if obedience has nothing to do with conforming to demands on your external behavior? What if obedience, at its core, is simple faith in the complete obedience of Jesus?

A. You don't have to struggle anymore

You can give up your struggle and simply rest in His finished work of obedience.

_____

_____

_____

The obedience of Jesus Christ has been accomplished for you and given to you by grace.

_____

_____

_____

The vicarious obedience of Christ frees you so that you can relax, listen to the melody of grace, and enjoy the dance, which is your life in Him. Religion requires, but grace inspires. Jesus offers us an invitation. "Are you tired? Worn out? Burned out on religion? Come to me. Get away with me and you'll recover your life. I'll show you how to take a real rest. Walk with me and work with me—watch how I do it. Learn the unforced rhythms of grace. I won't lay anything heavy or ill-fitting on you. Keep company with me and you'll learn to live freely and lightly. " (Matthew 11: 28-30 The Message)

B. Obedience Is a Dance

Your Dance Partner does dance perfectly, and He is leading you in this dance of grace called life.

_____

_____

_____

4. VICARIOUS REPENTANCE

Repentance is framed as a war against sinful thoughts, words, and deeds, drawing from the arsenal of sincere emotions and a ferocious will. Hit the sawdust trail and promise God you'll do better!! NO!

A. Why was Jesus baptized?

Jesus wasn't baptized because He needed to repent. He was being baptized for you and me.

_____

_____

His baptism of repentance was a vicarious baptism.

_____

_____

Repentance is a gift, not a discipline.

_____

_____

The word repentance actually denotes the act of changing one's mind.

_____

_____

Jesus Lived as Us

To genuinely repent is simply to align our belief with the work of Jesus Christ. If you trust Him, there is nothing more you need to do. There's nothing more you could do because He has already done it all. Repentance is nothing more than changing our minds about Him and what He has already done to deal with sin. Do you want to be sure you have fully repented of all your sins? Then see them as having been decimated and taken away by His finished work. That is New Covenant repentance.

B. Repentance Is a Way of Life

There is a sense in which our life in Christ is a lifetime of repentance—of changing our minds as He leads us out of the old, faulty belief systems we have held and brings us into an ever-increasing knowledge of the truth, which can be known only in Him.

_____

_____

_____

5. VICARIOUS FAITH

A. The challenge to have more faith about a specific outcome is often nothing more than a religious promotion for positive thinking.

_____

_____

_____

B. People experience authentic faith when their focus is on the Faithful One.

_____

_____

_____

C. Our faith originates from Him. Jesus is our Faith.

_____

_____

_____

D. Faith Is a Person

It is the faith of Christ that is ours. It is vicarious faith. He believes on our behalf, so all we need to do is trust Him.

_____

_____

_____

The basis of faith is God's faithfulness.

_____

_____

_____

In fact, there is no such thing as "my faith" because my faith is His faith, and His faith is based on His Father's faithfulness. The vicarious faith of Jesus Christ is your faith. What a relief!

ENCOUNTER YOUR REAL GOD

Jesus's earthly life was your life of obedience to the Father.
Obedience to God lives in you, and His name is Jesus.

Our life in Christ is a lifetime of repentance—of changing
our minds as He leads us out of the old, faulty belief systems
we have held and brings us
into an ever-increasing knowledge of the truth,
which can be known only in Him.

It is the faith of Christ that is ours. It is vicarious faith.
He believes on our behalf, so all we need to do is trust Him.

GRACE ISN'T FAIR

*The baseline of much religious conflict
boils down to one issue— how loving is our God?
Is He into payback or pardon or both?
This may be the most important question
you will ever answer because your viewpoint on this will affect everything.
It will frame how you view God, others, and even yourself.*

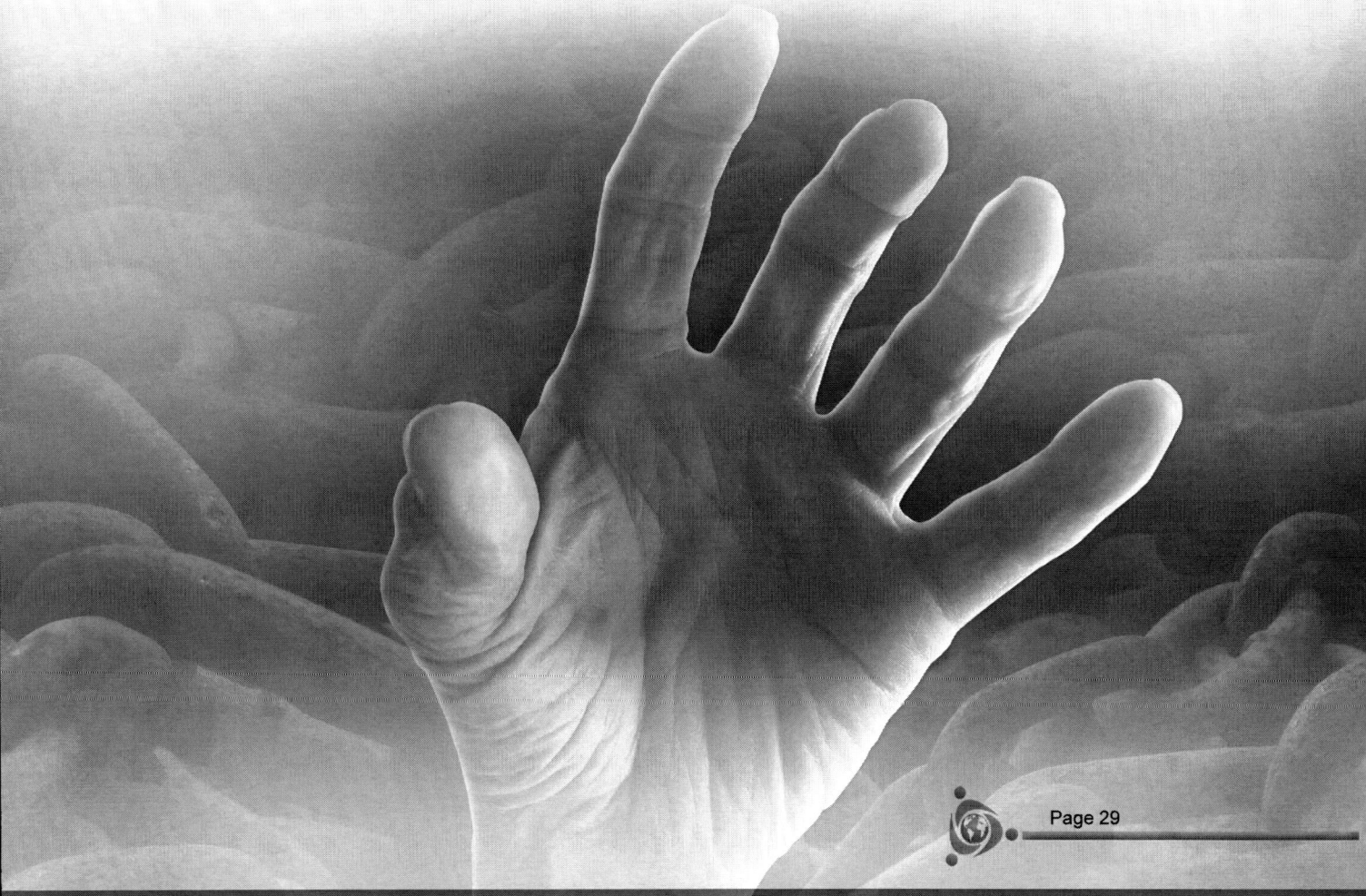

1. HARMONIZING JUSTICE WITH LOVE

We need to understand the words as they were used when they were written.

A. Legal Justice

It is solidly fixed in a system of law.

_____

_____

_____

It's the idea that when somebody does wrong, punishment is called for to make things right.

_____

_____

_____

If you try to fit God into this template, you will see Him as a divine courtroom Judge. Fairness will govern your whole concept of divine justice. Viewing Him through this lens, it will be easy to imagine Him as an angry God.

_____

_____

B. Restoration or Revenge?

There is, in fact, another understanding of justice, one that finds its roots in grace.

Not retribution but restoration. The goal in this expression of justice is to make the victim whole, to heal the offender and integrate him back into society as a productive person.

_____

_____

_____

Justice that originates in the God of love is redemptive.
    (Isaiah 30: 18, Zechariah 7: 9, Isaiah 1: 17, Jeremiah 21: 12)

_____

_____

_____

There is a higher way that expresses justice in grace. It's a way of restoration that lifts up and makes right the things that were wrong. Our Father is just to have forgiven our sin because Jesus righted the wrong done by Adam, and we all are the beneficiaries of His finished work.

GRACE IS A SCANDAL TO THE RELIGIOUS MIND!!

C. Moralism

That description is based on an expectation that came directly from the tree of the knowledge of good and evil.

_____

_____

_____

The insistence on fairness is really an admission of our own self-righteousness.

_____

_____

_____

Any qualifying requirement for grace destroys grace.

_____

_____

_____

D. Prodigals and Pious Sons

What our Father wants is us. He wants us to relax and simply enjoy our relationship to Him. Grace cannot connect with the one who promises to try harder. The nature of grace makes that impossible. It can connect only with those who have given up.

_____

_____

3. DID JESUS REALLY REVEAL THE FATHER?

A. The Christological Principle

_____

_____

B. A God like Jesus

Did Jesus leave out half the story, not telling us about the dark side of His Father?

_____

_____

To have a healthy and proper understanding of God, we must move beyond the idea that He is an angry, punitive magistrate who is more preoccupied with balancing the books than He is with us. Your Father is for you, and Jesus came to reveal that. There is no side to God the Father that looks different from the compassionate grace demonstrated by God the Son.

ENCOUNTER YOUR REAL GOD

Your God is not an angry divine courtroom judge
whose sense of justice requires that He pass verdict
and impose sentence on those who have done wrong.

Justice that originates in your God of love is redemptive.

Your God is for the restoration, not the retribution.

Any qualifying requirement for grace destroys grace.

In order to encounter your real God,
we must see every text of the Bible through the lens of Jesus.

Your Father is for you, and Jesus came to reveal that.

JESUS WASN'T FORSAKEN

What happened at the Cross?
What was the relationship between Jesus and His Father?
Did God the Father pour out His anger on Jesus
so He wouldn't have to punish us?
Did the Holy Spirit leave from Jesus?
Was Jesus forsaken?
What truly happened at the Cross?
The truth is both staggering and transformational.

1. HOW DID THE ATONEMENT WORK?

A. Traditional Approach

1. God is a God of justice and must act fairly in every matter.
2. Humanity has sinned and must be punished. Otherwise, God wouldn't be just.
3. Jesus loved us so much that He took our place on the cross, and God the Father poured out His anger on Jesus so He wouldn't have to punish us.
4. As a result, God the Father will forgive us for our sin if we will simply ask and trust Him to.

_____

_____

_____

B. The penal substitution theory of the atonement

The word "penal" indicates that the crucifixion was punishment by God the Father. Substitutionary points to the fact that Jesus took our place on the cross.

_____

_____

_____

This is the only way many have been taught about the cross, so they assume it is the only way to understand Jesus's crucifixion. Actually, that's not the case at all.

C. Other Theories

There are other theories that seek to understand the cross:

_____

_____

_____

2. THE INFLUENCE OF CULTURE

A. Your method for understanding what the Bible says has been guided by your culture and by those who have helped shape it.

It isn't a question of what the Bible says. The question is, What does the Bible mean by what it says?

_____

_____

We must rise above the cultural blindness in order to grow in grace.

Two leaders who had tremendous influence in the early church left an imprint that still impacts us today. The Western church leaned toward Augustine's interpretation of the atonement, and the Eastern church emphasized Athanasius's teaching.

_____

_____

_____

B. Two Perspectives

An Augustinian approach to sharing the gospel usually begins with the problem of sin, and then it progresses toward the solution in the cross.

_____

_____

_____

Athanasius's tack started with the love of our triune God for those He created, and then it moves toward humanity's need.

_____

_____

_____

In reality, the Father, Son, and Holy Spirit were all involved in rescuing us from sin's penalty. (Hebrews 9: 14 says that Jesus offered Himself through the eternal Spirit. The Spirit empowered Jesus, the Son of Man, to do what He did.)

Jesus Wasn't Forsaken

3. SEPARATION ANXIETY

A. The Three-in-One is one in essence.

If it's not the Three-in-One, it is not the true and living God.

_____

_____

_____

If the Father separated from Jesus on the cross, literally forsaking Him and refusing to live in oneness with Him, the Trinity didn't exist at that moment. How could God exist if His unified, triune essence was undone? Considering that God is a Trinity, it would then be accurate to say that God no longer existed when Jesus was on the cross. God is no longer God? What an absurdity!

B. God in a Sinful World

Jesus saw sin as a fatal disease that needed to be cured, not a legal violation that He needed to punish.

Where did this idea that God can't look on sin begin?

_____

_____

_____

Habakkuk 1: 13

_____

_____

_____

God didn't tell Habakkuk that He couldn't look on evil. Instead, Habakkuk was venting his pain and confusion through his own theology.

_____

_____

_____

C. So was Jesus forsaken by His Father?

Jesus felt abandoned by God the Father.

_____

_____

_____

So don't condemn yourself for having negative emotions at times when you face problems in life.

_____

_____

Psalm 22 is one of the most easily understood psalms about Jesus because its meaning is so obvious.

_____

_____

_____

"My God, my God, why have You forsaken me?" Verse 24 gives a clear answer to the question. "For He has not despised nor abhorred the affliction of the afflicted; Nor has He hidden His face from him; But when he cried to Him for help, He heard."

JESUS WASN'T FORSAKEN BY HIS FATHER!!!

This clear answer in Psalm 22: 24 can empower you to change your mind about the matter and move beyond an angry God to an understanding of your loving Father as He really is and always has been.

4. OLD TESTAMENT TYPES

Examine every reference to sacrifices under the Mosaic system in the Old Testament, and you will not find a shred of evidence of anger or a single reference to punishment. No anger or cruelty was intended or expressed in the process. The sacrifice was effective because of the blood of the lamb, not because of any violence, anger, or punishment.

A. The Scapegoat

_____

_____

_____

Just as Aaron wasn't angry when he laid his hands on the head of the goat, neither was our Father angry when Jesus took away the sins of the world. (See Hebrews 9: 26)

_____

_____

_____

B. The Sin Offering

_____

_____

_____

Jesus's sacrifice didn't cause His Father to turn away in disgust— it was actually a beautiful smell that brought the Father great joy as He witnessed the selflessness of His Son.

_____

_____

_____

7. A TROUBLING TRADITION

Consider the word forgiveness. It doesn't have to have the judicial meaning we often assume it does. It can also mean "to take away."

The Hebrew word *nasa* means, "to pick up something up and carry it away."

_____

The Greek word *aphiemi* means, "to send or make go away."

_____

The Greek word *charizomai* denotes, "the action of doing something pleasant, gracious, and benevolent toward another person."

_____

Divine forgiveness is the gracious act of sending our sins away from us and never associating them with us again. If the Father didn't punish Jesus on the cross, does that mean there is no punishment for sin? Sin brings its own punishment.

ENCOUNTER YOUR REAL GOD

In reality, the Father, Son, and Holy Spirit
were all involved in rescuing us from sin's penalty.

Jesus only felt as if God the Father had abandoned Him.
Your God the Father did not pour out His anger on Jesus!

God the Father never forsook His Son on the cross,
but was with Him the whole time.

The Father didn't punish Jesus on the cross.
Sin brings its own punishment.

GOD ISN'T ANGRY

*From the time Adam sinned and hid himself in the Garden of Eden,
people have had the mistaken notion
that God was coming to exact revenge on them
for their wrongdoing. When we begin to see our Father
through the eyes of grace, we understand that the cross wasn't a courtroom.
Rather, Jesus sacrificed Himself for us by taking our sin into Himself
so we could be healed from its deadly effect.*

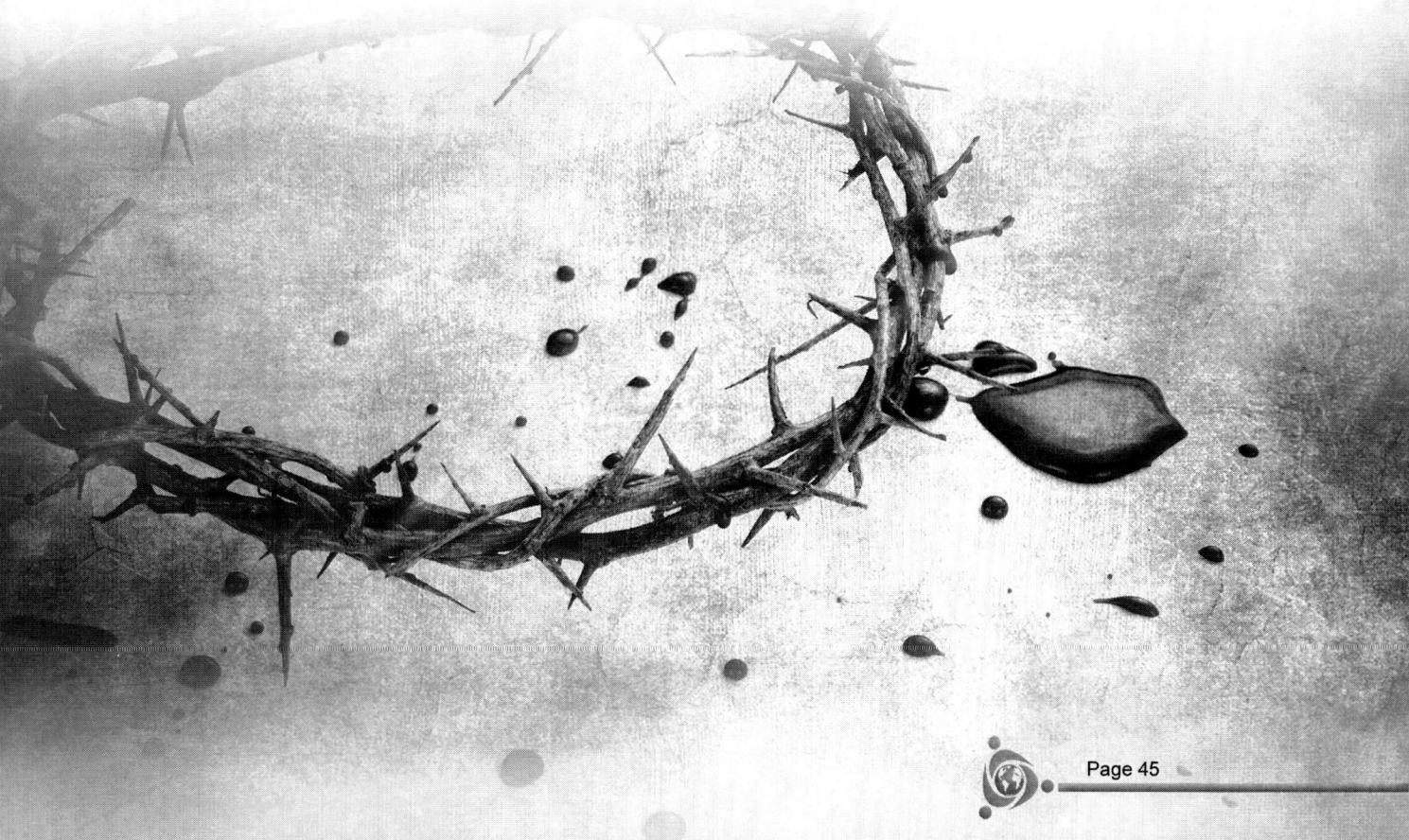

1. REMEDY OR RETRIBUTION?

The cross was the New Covenant substance foreshadowed by the Old Covenant mercy seat.

_____

_____

_____

Propitiation was remedial, not retributive! The cross was the place of divine agape, not divine anger!

_____

_____

_____

2. THE CROSS DEALT WITH SINS

A. Christus Victor Theory

_____

_____

_____

_____

B. Satisfaction Theory

_____

_____

_____

C. Penal Substitution Theory

_____

_____

_____

3. THE CROSS DEALT WITH SINNERS

A. At the cross, Jesus put away humanity's sin.

_____

_____

_____

B. Jesus took on Adamic humanity, drawing it into Himself on the cross so we would die with Him.

_____

_____

C. Who else was included — only believers, or does this act of Jesus on the cross include everybody? (2 Corinthians 5: 14-15)

_____

_____

_____

D. Did Jesus die for all types of people or for each and every person? He died for every person!
(See Hebrews 2.9, 2 Corinthians 5)

_____

_____

_____

4. WHEN DID SINFUL HUMANITY DIE?

A. When did this happen? Does it happen when a person trusts Christ by faith? No, it doesn't. It happened at the cross.

_____

_____

_____

You and your decision didn't cause your co-crucifixion with Christ. Jesus and His finished work accomplished that. A Christian is a believer in Jesus Christ. Rather, it means that the success of the finished work of Jesus Christ on the cross doesn't depend on human beings casting a vote in His favor.

Watchman Nee said, "It is the inclusive death of the Lord which puts me in a position to identify myself, not that I identify myself in order to be included . It is God's inclusion of me in Christ that matters."

B. The Role of Faith

Through faith, the invisible reality that already exists becomes our visible experience. Through faith, the objective reality becomes our subjective realization.

_____

_____

_____

To proclaim the gospel is to tell people that it really is finished.
To experience salvation is to believe it and live from the reality of His work on our behalf.

C. Did Christ Succeed? (See Romans 5.6-11)

_____

_____

_____

The Bible says the reconciling work of Christ happened while humanity was helpless, while we were sinners, and while we were enemies.

5. WHAT IS OUR RESPONSE?

A. Simply acknowledge the love and forgiveness God has bestowed on us and accept it.

_____

_____

_____

B. You have been reconciled to God, so stop resisting Him and be reconciled to Him. In other words, own it and live in the freedom of divine acceptance and forgiveness of sin.

_____

_____

_____

SO...WHY DO WE SIN?

If Jesus did that for the whole world, why do people still sin? Adam didn't have a sin nature before the fall in the Garden of Eden. Why did he sin? The reason Adam sinned and the reason people still sin today (both believers and unbelievers) is simple. They believe a lie. What is this lie? It is the lie that we can meet our own needs by relying on ourselves instead of living in dependence on our God. It is the lie that independence is a good thing. It is the lie that sinful behavior is gratifying and personally beneficial for those who sin.

6. GOD'S WRATH

Wrath usually refers to anger, but it can also refer to any violent emotion. Wrath can have to do with passionate eagerness just as it does anger. (Greek word *Orge*)

_____

_____

_____

ENCOUNTER YOUR REAL GOD

The cross was the place of divine *agape*, not divine anger!

Jesus put away the sins humanity committed at the cross.

Jesus didn't simply die for us; He also died as us.
When He died, Adam's race died with Him. We all died with Him.

The reason Adam sinned and the reason people still sin today
(both believers and unbelievers) is simple. They believe a lie.

God did what He did for you before you could do a thing
or could even want to.
He has received you, so relax and rest in His acceptance.
You have been reconciled to your God, so stop resisting Him
and be reconciled to Him. In other words,
own it and live in the freedom of divine acceptance and forgiveness of sin.
Your God loves you so much!!

HIS FAITH CHANGED EVERYTHING

*Do We Need to Believe? What Jesus did on the cross for all humanity
is a reality that doesn't depend on our acknowledgment to be true.
It's true whether we believe it or not.
However— and this is important—until we believe the gospel,
it will have no effect on our personal experience. (See Hebrews 4.2)*

1. WHOSE FAITH?

A. Adam Isn't Bigger than Jesus

_____

_____

_____

B. Forgiveness and Faith

Did the Jewish person for whom the priest offered the sacrifice have to have faith in the sacrifice for his sins to be forgiven?

_____

_____

_____

Jesus was the perfect sacrifice who offered Himself for us before we could even respond with either faith or rejection. (See Hebrews 9: 26)

_____

_____

_____

C. Jesus's Faith has Justified Us

_____

_____

_____

D. Considering Two Small Words – In and Of

To be justified by faith in Christ is very different from being justified by the faith of Christ. One depends on our faith, and the other rests in His faith.

_____

_____

_____

Do these verses suggest that the necessary faith originates with God or with man?

Romans 3.22 _____

_____

Galatians 2.16 _____

_____

Galatians 2.20 _____

_____

Not an egocentric approach, but a Christocentric ("Christ centered") principle

_____

_____

_____

E. Consistency Is Key

Romans 3: 26

_____

_____

_____

Romans 4: 16

_____

_____

_____

F. His Faith Becomes Our Faith.

_____

_____

2. OBJECTIVE AND SUBJECTIVE ASPECTS OF THE GOSPEL

A. Our faith is the activation of His faith in and through us.

"One Lord, one faith, one baptism" (Ephesians 4: 5).

_____

_____

_____

Romans 1.17 teaches it is, "from faith to faith." What does that mean? It means that the faith of Jesus becomes our faith.

_____

_____

_____

B. None Are Left Out

The atoning work of Christ doesn't affect us simply because we believe it. It affects everybody whether we believe it or not. That is what makes the gospel so exciting. No one is excluded in the cross. All mankind was in Him on that horrible and wonderful day. When Jesus died, it was His faith (or to fine tune it even more, His faithfulness) that solved Adam's problem. All humanity was gathered up in Him, and in His death, we all died.

C. Chosen Before We Believed

Ephesians 1: 4

_____

_____

_____

Your origin in Him precedes time and space, reaching all the way into eternity.

_____

_____

_____

Everybody and everything is in Him. Nothing exists or happens outside Him.

_____

_____

Because in him were the all things created, those in the heavens, and those upon the earth, those visible, and those invisible, whether thrones, whether lordships, whether principalities, whether authorities; all things through him, and for him, have been created, and himself is before all, and the all things in him have consisted. (Colossians 1:16-17, Young's Literal Translation)

D. Living a Lie

There is no distance between God and man.

_____

_____

Without knowing the truth, humanity's default setting is to live the lie. Unbelievers are living out of a lie and not walking in the truth.

_____

_____

E. God's Work Came First

We are reconciled and that is why we can be reconciled.
(See 2 Corinthians 5: 19-20)

_____

_____

The effect of the cross did not change the heart of God, but the heart of man.

_____

This reconciliation He accomplished is the exchanged life. The biblical use of the word reconciled denotes the idea of exchanging coins for other coins of equivalent value. The full message of the exchanged life is that Jesus has exchanged the life of all of humanity with His own. (Romans 5.10)

ENCOUNTER YOUR REAL GOD

Adam's sin certainly was not greater than Christ's life and death.

It's Jesus's faith that has justified us. It's not our own faith
that we have placed in Him.

Our faith is the activation of Jesus' faith in and through us.

The faith of Jesus becomes our faith.

There is no distance between your God and all of us.
Any perception of distance is an illusion.

The effect of the cross did not change the heart of your God,
but the heart of man. It was man who needed to be reconciled, not God.

The full message of the exchanged life is
that Jesus has exchanged the life of all of humanity with His own.

NOT YOUR GRANDMOTHER'S HELL

*We don't need to scare people into heaven. Jesus will be enough to attract them.
Salvation isn't about heaven and hell. It's about knowing our Father
through His Son in the Holy Spirit.(John 17.3)
The threat of hell is the approach often used in evangelism
by folks who have never clearly seen
the beauty of Jesus. Our understanding of hell
must be filtered through the lens of the love of our God.*

1. THE CURRENT CONVERSATION

Can we believe hell exists and embrace the reality of a God who isn't angry and who can never do anything less than to love?

_____

_____

_____

Infernalism and Annihilationism

_____

_____

_____

Ask the average churchgoer today to describe what hell is like, and you'll likely get a description that sounds much like Dante Alighieri's fictional account of hell in Inferno, one of three poems he wrote in The Divine Comedy.

We can fully believe in the love of God without rejecting the whole idea of hell.

Not Your Grandmother's Hell

1. A PLACE AND A CONDITION

A. Two Important Words

Greek word *Hades* or the Hebrew word *Sheol*

_____

_____

_____

Gehenna

_____

_____

_____

How can hell be real if God really is pure love? How could He even allow such a thing? How can one argue that God isn't an angry God, if hell is real? How do the two fit together?

B. Is Hell Outside of God?

The most prevalent teaching about hell is that it is a place where God is absent.

_____

_____

_____

Nothing exists that is not created and sustained by the Creator. (See Colossians 1: 15-17).

_____

_____

_____

If God is omnipresent, He cannot be absent from hell.

_____

_____

_____

C. The Presence of God

The phrase, "away from the presence of the LORD," doesn't mean that God isn't there. It refers to a place of rebellion where people can't experience God's loving blessings because of their attitude, not His.

_____

_____

_____

Not Your Grandmother's Hell

1. THE FIRE OF HELL

A. "Our God is a consuming fire." (Hebrews 12: 29)

_____

_____

_____

God is fire. God is love. Therefore, that fire is love. Would your view of hell change if the fire were actually the experience of those in eternity who still loathe God as they are engulfed in the flames of divine love?

B. Torment and Love

What if the torment experienced by those who still despise God is actually the inescapable presence of His love?

_____

_____

_____

Can His love be experienced as fire? (See Exodus 24: 16-18)

_____

_____

_____

Sinners and saints experience the same fire. The first group would be terrified, but the latter group had nothing to fear.

_____

_____

Eternity doesn't have zip codes. (See Daniel 7.10)

_____

_____

C. An Interpretation with Deep Roots

In the Eastern Church's way of thinking, God is the fire that we experience as either a blessing or a torment, depending on our spiritual state.

_____

_____

"Love's power acts in two ways: it torments sinners, while at the same time it delights those who have lived in accord with it."
- *Seventh-century theologian and bishop Isaac the Assyrian*

4. HOPE

The last chapter of the Bible leaves the matter open-ended.
(Revelation 22: 15-17)

ENCOUNTER YOUR REAL GOD

The most prevalent teaching about hell is that it is a place
where your God is absent.
If God is omnipresent, He cannot be absent from hell.

Hebrews 12: 29: "Our God is a consuming fire." Your God is fire.
Your God is love. Therefore, that fire is love.
Your God is passionate about you!
Your God passionately loves you!

Hell is the inescapable presence of God's love
surrounding those who detest that Love.

Sinners and saints experience the same fire.
The first group would be terrified, but the latter group had nothing to fear.

FINAL REMARKS

Our faulty or shortsighted concepts are being taken away from us to make room for a bigger picture. That can be uncomfortable to say the least. Moving from the known to the unknown to the Known, from light to darkness to the Light, is integral to the grace walk.

If you truly want to grow in grace, it is important to remember that having all the answers doesn't necessarily mean we have reached His goal for us. To the contrary, He is more interested in our journey and how we trust, follow, and obey Him along the way. God is not a puzzle to be solved. He is Mystery to be explored. Sometimes the heart knows before the head catches up with the truth.

God's Love Changes Everything!! Have you settled in your own mind on the reality of God's absolute love? Do you still find yourself grappling with whether love is just one of His qualities alongside others? If you want to grow in grace and live in peace, you must settle the answer to this question.

Once we have moved beyond an angry God and met Him as He is, we have discovered the single greatest key for navigating the ups and downs of life. No matter what happens, if we know that Love Personified is sovereign over the affairs of life, we will find in Him the tenacity to face any situation.

Seeing Others Through His Eyes. From now on everyone is defined by Christ, everyone is included in Christ. Unbelievers most assuredly need to trust Christ. Apart from that subjective experience, they will always be like the older brother in the story of the prodigal son.

There is No Insiders or Outsiders. There is NO Us versus Them!! Loving people—that's what it's all about in this world.

The gospel message, however, is that we all are included in Him and what He has done on our behalf. Accept it and be blessed. This gospel we proclaim isn't a message of what can be but is the good news of what already is in Jesus Christ.

For more information about available resources
to help you grow in your own grace walk, please visit

www.gracewalkresources.com

To learn more about Grace Walk, please visit our web site at

www.gracewalk.org

Beyond an Angry God

Conference

Manufactured by Amazon.ca
Acheson, AB

13059480R00039